REMNANTS

of a LIFE

Poems
by

Duane L. Herrmann

Lighted Lake Press

Remnants of a Life: Poems

Copyright © 2019 by Duane L. Herrmann

All rights reserved.

ISBN 13: 978-0-9969627-1-1

Library of Congress Control Number (LCCN): 2019914883

Lighted Lake Press

Topeka, KS

Author's note:

Many of these are poems I refused to gather and publish together while my mother was alive. I had eventually come to realize that she was totally unaware of the damage she caused to others, and unable to accept it. She would have been bewildered, at least, by the accounts related here. She left wreckage in her wake which I am still processing. All events related here are accurate to my memory, except the first, that is merely an imaginary possibility.

Welcome to my life.

dlh…

CONTENTS

Fire Exposed	5
It Is…	6
Marvelous Beast!	7
Stars	9
Pony Express	10
Intersection	11
First Step	12
Silent Teacher	13
Green Haze	14
God Created	15
Countless Strangers Passing	16
Tree Friends	17
Beginning Again	18
Ticks Don't Swim	20
Found	21
This Blood	22
Native Roots	23
Native Proud	24
Passing By	25
Hidden in Plain Sight	26
On The Central Plain	27
Frontier Trail	28
Emil Driving	29
Fossiliferous House	30
Oven Walking	31
Walking High	32
Dinner Guest	33
Master and the Dog	34
Chopping Fingers	35

Table Manner	36
Dreamer Boy	37
Wringer Takes All	38
Kitchen Comfort	39
Nightly Refuge	40
Oh, Please!	41
Killer Boy	43
This Pet, "No."	44
Sweet Relief	45
Choking Hazard	46
That One Night	47
Bereavement	49
Tomato Confession	50
Beginning and the End	51
Boy with Marbles	53
Twice	54
Finale	56
Rest in Peace	58
One Long Night	59
Screaming Monster Dragon	60
Poet	61
Wind in Trees	62
Memories Be	63
House Doors	64
There's a Chicken!	65
A Father's Love	66
The Wasp	68
A Rabbit Goes	69
Summer Adventure	70
Butterfly Tracks	71
Rain People	72

On Highway 50	73
Birdwatching at Sunrise	74
Bright Light	75
Angelic Source	76
Rejoicing	77
Dead Bridge	78
Remnant	79
Rock Walls	80
Windmills Side by Side	81
Autumn Stillness	82
Under Water Life	83
Plains Change	84
Protecting Boards	85
Autumn Flaming Sky	86
Northward	87
Feeding Cattle	88
Road Game	89
Wind Rehearsal	90
Snow Dusting	91
World Transformed	92
Sitting Time	93
Snowy Hike	94
Differing	95
He Wonders	96
Spirit Waits	97
Bay Fortified	98
Aftermath	99
McDonald Sheep Ranch	100
Collapse of Civilization	102
Armenian Witness	103
Akhmatova	105
Poem Fruit	106

Yezhof Winter	107
A Sacrifice	108
Me and Melanin	109
Against the Dark	110
Alone in His Mind	111
Whispers Washing	112
Chocolate Bliss	113
The End is Near	114
Just Beyond	115
Elephant Response	117
Building Words	118
Blessed is the Place	119
Owl Calling	121
Imaginary Life	122
Finding Earth	123
And, the Word…	124
Notes and Sources	127
Index of Titles	131
Index of First Lines	135
Previously published credits	139
Other Books by Duane L. Herrmann	141
About the Author	142

poems

FIRE EXPOSED

On a clear, still day
fire swept through,
a legal one –
springtime burning,
pasture was now cleaned.
From a gully
a stream of smoke,
some log,
or pile of brush,
still burning.
The farmer checked
and his surprise
found smoldering
on the ground
cloth,
remnants of clothes,
on a body
still.

IT IS…

Chainsaw hanging from a tree
like an ornament
but not!

MARVELOUS BEAST!

"Incognitum,"
   the unknown species
that roamed the earth
   before The Flood,
PROOF
   what the Bible said is true.
Or, so it seemed
   in 1705
when a five pound tooth
   was found
in the Hudson River Valley
   near Claverack.
Cotton Mather preached
   on the beast
and its demise
   at the hand of an angry God.
A hundred years before dinosaurs
   would be discovered,
this monstrous beast
   captured the imagination
of Americans
   as their own Great Thing!

>

Today we know
   it was a mastodon,
not mammoth
   as mistaken for.
The incognitum
   was awesome to behold,
with the bones assembled,
   but backward tusks,
and a dinner party
   held beneath!
"Might some still be
   in the unknown west?"
Mused the President
   who sent Lewis and Clark to look.

STARS

The brilliance and generosity
of stars spangled
across the sky:
night would be so bleak
without them –
a void of black.
What imagination
would then soar?
Chart the seas?
Tell tales
of heroes and deeds?
If this planet circled far,
far from the center of space,
with no stars,
the conscious creatures
would not thrive
and civilization
expire.

PONY EXPRESS

Small young men,
   fast ponies
to carry mail
   between the ends
of eastern and western
   rail lines
over empty prairie
   and mountains.
They ran flying
   in relays
to move the mail
   in the shortest time.
Only nineteen months
   this business ran
until telegraph wires
   were strung,
yet in that time
   legends had begun.

INTERSECTION

Past and present cross,
two streams of time:
Pony Express Trail
and Kansas Highway
159!
Not expecting connection
the driver sees
this link
of now and then:
those boys once
rode
into the future
and our memory
as I drive
into mine.
Where –
   are they now?
Where will I be?

FIRST STEP

Airborne, independently,
the first step,
launching,
fragile, impractical, impossible,
of the human race.

Twelve seconds,
twelve more,
then fifteen;
finally one minute:
confirmation
that flight WAS possible.

On 17 December 1903
we became an airborne species
and, less than four score later,
landed on the moon.
In the lifetime of many:
earthbound to space-faring.

Who would believe...?

SILENT TEACHER

Orange orb
silent rising
from the land
witness to
eons and ages
of human history
and so much before.
Primitives gazed in wonder
and awe,
and some prayed.
Later men adored.
Later still, we walked
and will some day
live and work
and travel far.
It pulled us up,
taught respect,
and sent us to the stars.

GREEN HAZE

Spring's arrival has begun:
over countryside and town
the green haze of spring
has appeared.
And wind
through new growth
is different
than bare branches.
Trees
putting forth buds and leaves
are evidence
of a new
year beginning.
Air is warm
and birds,
songs in the air,
are starting
to return.

GOD CREATED

Sex starved females
   will suck your blood if they can.

Their siren song is meant to distract
   but gives you a chance
   for a spirited defense.

Damn mosquitoes!

Where do they fit in God's plan?

COUNTLESS STRANGERS PASSING

This farm I see distantly
from the highway
slicing through fields –
what did the farmer feel
when he learned,
one day long ago,
this road
would cut through
his family land?
He had no choice
but submit
to powers greater
than his own –
and precious fields,
dismembered, graded, paved,
for convenience
of countless strangers passing
through his pain.

TREE FRIENDS

Tree branches
waving
smiling
pulling
whispering –
to me.
My friends…
My comfort…
My hope.
Strong trunks move
in the wind
but do not yield
until compelled by force.
Trees shelter
life
of all kinds,
in, near and around.
Human generations
a tree stands
sheltering all.
A tree is a world,
an island
on the prairie,
for shade.
A tree finds me
and I find…
a friend.

BEGINNING AGAIN

New moon…
New month…
New beginning…
Regularity…
A chance to start over
every few weeks
for those
who can't get it right
the first time,
second time,
third time…
Who's counting?
I keep trying,
several decades now,
I don't count them either:
too much to do
so little time
life is short.
I must do all I can
with each breath.

>

One day
I'll be done counting
the sum will be added
to a life full-lived,
and the balance, or…

at least:
I tried.

TICKS DON'T SWIM

Not only do they not swim
they don't float
or even tread water:
they sink.
Once a tick's in water
it's no threat to you,
so, go ahead,
flick that tick
into water, any water:
toilet bowl,
running drain,
dog dish,
swimming pool, or even
your own drink.
Don't worry
the tick will sink
and you will be
free! Free! FREE!!

FOUND

Bones in the meadow lie
after the fire to burn dead grass.
It was a cow, the skull says,
the lost one – missing
some time last summer
and just now found.
The farmer paused…
This cow…
Was she the stubborn one?
Or, the one who ran away?
Obviously
she did not like the herd,
or, did the herd
reject her?
It's over now,
the life, the missing.
What do we do now
with the bones?

THIS BLOOD

Through these veins
flow Native blood
of this land
for millennia.
What accomplishments
was she descendent from?
Cahokia?
Tenochtitlan?
Machu Picchu?
Or, humbler lives
living with the earth
and keeping culture
until invaders came.
I cannot know her
or from whence she came,
but I can honor
her life and people
never knowing more.

NATIVE ROOTS

My mother's father
   could have been
a member of the tribe,
   if the tribe
accepted great grandchildren
   of full bloods,
But we don't know
   their names,
not even
   which tribe,
nor where
   the tribe was from.
No records kept,
   nor honor given
to native ancestors,
   our native roots.

My history
   has been erased.

NATIVE PROUD

Ancestor
   whose name I do not know
and whose tribe
   I'm equally unaware,
Yet, in my blood
   your echo flows –
great great great
   grandparent of mine.
How can I know
   who I am, completely,
when I do not know
   who you are:
your tribe,
   your hunting grounds,
ceremonies,
   beliefs and life?
I am incomplete, but proud
   of my native blood!

PASSING BY

Sleeping peacefully one night
   in my blanket on the ground
(my home had been burned,
   by some whites, I suppose),
I was dreaming of a time
   when I taught my white friend
how to hunt
   and find food on his own,
when a white man
   (I saw him walk away)
saw a "red skin"
   and did his duty for his race.
Proud of his cowardly act
   but ignorant
of the Great Creator Spirit
   and the value of life
as he quite surely put
   a bullet through my head.

HIDDEN IN PLAIN SIGHT

Hills overgrown with trees
   no evidence
is visible
   of civilization
and yet, hidden deep
   within the mounds
lie remains
   of a great and mighty civilization
unknown to later generations
   of conquerors and conquered.
Secrets of the sun and stars
   embedded and acknowledged
in their observatory
   of cosmic intelligence.
Knowledge and culture
   all
now swept away
   and obliterated.

ON THE CENTRAL PLAIN

Peak afternoon heat,
   not the smartest time,
for a summer hike,
   but homage I paid
and reverence
   to the ancient ones.
Ignorant of ceremonies
   and the language,
yet I come with respect
   to this holy place:
this mound, rising
   from the vast, open plain,
a remnant city
   of once vast and
mighty civilization
   with secrets unknown
hundreds of years now
   vanished.

FRONTIER TRAIL

Traffic has passed on:
activity and earnestness,
desperation, effort;
all vanished now.
A faint line
prairie winding
shows the way,
and only hints
of memory remain.

EMIL DRIVING

He was a farmer
   driving horses
in the quiet
   of the fields,
birds broke the silence
   or a distant dog.
"Gee" and "Haw,"
   "gehen" und "halt,"
words he knew,
   the horses too
for they had farmed
   already more then he:
now learning Englisch;
   born in Amerika,
but still German;
   in 1912, Emil Lutz
began farming at
   six years old!

FOSSILIFEROUS HOUSE

My grandmother's house
is built of fossils:
remains
of ancient life.
As a child I would stare
and trace the lines
in the stones
that once were bones.
Rock for this house
was carved from the land,
once the floor
of Pennsylvania Sea.
Tiny fossils
like bits of fingernails,
source of wonder
and amazement;
I learned early:
Earth will change.

OVEN WALKING

Walking in the oven
one hundred plus
degrees
with heat index
even higher,
but work I must
for time is short
and the killing
must continue.
If leaves aren't dead
for at least a month
to starve the roots
then all the effort
is in vain.
So, I go
in the heat
and kill, kill, kill
brush invading the meadow.

WALKING HIGH

Above the fence,
old and stone,
with moss,
I see clouds
silent,
majestic ships
sailing along,
flotilla
stretching far,
and below my feet:
dirt with life –
plants, microbes,
and more,
busy, busy, busy
creating, generating,
and growing
all around me:
the world in process,
continuing
and I sing
of the glory
of all things!
And, for reprise,
I shout
exaltation
to the Heavens
of Glory!

DINNER GUEST

He knew he was
   a member of the family
having been raised
   since shortly after birth;
he grew and thrived
   on love and attention.
No picky eater,
   past the eye dropper stage,
he ate almost the same
   as the rest of the family,
and he surely
   loved to eat!
It was fun at dinner
   as he walked
from lap to lap
   under the table
as we fed our guest –
   pet raccoon!

MASTER AND THE DOG

When the Master has a stick,
    and beats and beats and beats
and beats the dog,
    how greatly will the dog
want to be near the master?
    The desire may exist,
but the dog will know:
    the beating WILL come.
The beating is a fact
    of the dog's life.
So when the dog has a choice
    it will not long
remain at the master's side,
    for as much as it desires
to be with the master
    the dog has learned
that it must stay away;
    so I too, avoid my mother.

CHOPPING FINGERS

Unable to write
her anger rose –
the ink pen refills
did not write,
though newly bought
the ink had dried.
Even boiling
did not soften.
In rage she spread
them on a board,
seized the butcher knife
and whacked them up
screaming all the while.
Her little children saw
finger-like forms
and shuddered
at what her rage
might do to them.

TABLE MANNER

In silent protest:
the food came up.
He did not want to eat it.

Startling all
she grabbed the clean jar
and caught every drop.

Then she made him drink it.

The next time
she didn't bother with a jar
but clamped her hand
on his small mouth.
He gagged
but swallowed it again.

Sometimes,
it is still hard for the man
to swallow.

DREAMER BOY

Farm boy sits in grass
reading
of another life,
another time,
another world.
Who might he
someday be?
Gentle breeze whispers,
"You too can do."
He begins to hope
for a time when he can,
when his life
becomes his own,
not bound
by others' expectations.
For now, he reads –
and dreams.

WRINGER TAKES ALL

"Do not leave children
unattended
when machine
is in use,"
for good reason.
Children learn by doing
even if
the action will cause harm.

I was age ten or so,
alone doing laundry
when I wanted to know
what the wringer felt like:

Its grip was relentless.
I panicked.
Just before my elbow, I realized
I could turn it to reverse,
and did so –
thus saved my life.

KITCHEN COMFORT

The boy, not yet a teen,
washing dishes,
not by choice, but ordered,
stacks upon stacks of dishes.
He hated it all – dreaming
to be anywhere else and free!

WHAM!

Pain back of his head.
He gripped the sink to stand
and felt faint.
"Head's thicker'n I thought,"
giggled mother in surprise.
"No wonder he's dense;
he cracked it!"
The family serving platter,
solid for generations,
now middle cracked:
weapon of felony assault.

NIGHTLY REFUGE

After day, unending
working, working, working,
with screamed instructions,
criticism
and more screams,
little boy collapses
in bed at night
his refuge,
almost safe,
there, in dark,
he creates
his own worlds,
his own adventures:
stories in his mind,
his salvation
to validate
and compensate
his experience.

OH, PLEASE!

"Don't-let-it-come-to-me,
don't-let-it-come-to-me,
don't-let-it-come-to-me.
PLEASE, God!
Don't-let-it-come to ME!"

He stood, bewildered
and in dread,
some unidentifiable where
in that vast space
they called
"the outfield."
Not by choice.
Where was the comfort-security
of the Library
and books?
But this was P.E.
and baseball
was no choice.
The sun was hot
and birds sang, "away…"

"Don't-let-it-come-to-me,
don't-let-it-come to meee…"

\>

The eternal inning
was eventually over
and he could finally
leave. Gratefully,
the ball   never   came.

KILLER BOY

By age twelve
I was expert killer:
one clean slice
through the neck,
they didn't feel a thing,
toss the body aside –
on to the next,
blood didn't bother.
Some would spasm,
others tried to run
but not for long.
I was good –
took success in stride.
It was a family pattern,
we had to kill.

Without the killing:
no fried chicken
for Sunday dinner!

THIS PET, "NO."

Skunks mid night
   were let loose
with children
   fast asleep.
Mother did not
   trust them.
"They can be fixed,"
   the father urged,
he was the one
   who brought them home.
"No, they go,"
   she drew the line:
raccoons, pigs,
   and baby chicks
enough
   to share the house;
so deep one night
   they waddled out of sight.

SWEET RELIEF

Explosion of glass
release tension inside
me!

<u>SMASH</u>!! <u>CRASH</u>!!

Broken glass.

Sweet relief
washes over
me.
I can now think,
calmly plan
and attend
to urgent, other, needs.
Rage and Panic
flowed away –
mind is clear now
and, hopefully,
I can make it
one more day!

CHOKING HAZARD

Middle aged woman
chokes
on food in café.
Nearly adult son
laughs,
recognizes crisis
yet can't help.
Others stare in disbelief.
He knows he should help
but can't.
For the first time
his abusive
dominating mother
is not in control.
He'd never imagined it:
his lifetime
of helpless pain
reversed.

THAT ONE NIGHT

An acquaintance
far from home
needed to sleep,
was offered the room
next to mine.
I, a naïve teen,
uninformed, unaware,
socially innocent;
he, twice my age
and that much heavier,
offered a massage,
curious, I accepted.
Midway through
objected to my undershorts –
I removed them.
In moving over me
I felt he had none too.
Then he poked
and asked for lube.
I froze, paralyzed,
unable to move or speak.
"You want it rough then,"
he chuckled and began.

>

What?!
I felt the handle
of a rake, or hoe, or shovel
going in and out –
it hurts! It HURTS!
OH GOD, it HURTS!!!

Finished, he got off,
kissed my back,
then went to bed.

Next morning he
was cheerful –
I could not speak,
still felt him in me.

BEREAVEMENT

Yes,
my granddaughter's dead,
we'll bury her tomorrow,
do you want to see
the cakes I've made
and decorated?
I have the book
of pictures here…
Look!
This wedding cake
was my best...
And, this cake
I made
for the politician who…

MOM!

Oh,
I have to go.
My son is crying.

TOMATO CONFESSION

Who, but a sibling,
can understand
and appreciate
the confessional status
of a tomato sandwich:
bread, mayo and tomato;
that's it –
yet far too deviant
from the classic BLT
to be thought acceptable
to a mother who delighted
in castigating any,
but especially her children,
for anything which differed
from her expectations.

Making, and eating,
a tomato sandwich
was a furtive crime.

BEGINNING AND THE END

Two boys
both tied to the land
and to each other
but strangers.
The Beginning and the End
see life
from different directions.
And it is different
but somewhat same.
Sameness is deceptive:
same hills and fields
are different worlds
with different lives.
The same parent
was a different person
for different reasons.
How can two boys
see each other
standing on each other
in different worlds?
The End and the Beginning
have the same need
to be in the open grass
and trees
with different aims.

>

The Beginning and the End
can't talk much:
their words loaded with pain.
The End and the Beginning
cannot see each other
for the distance.
The Beginning and the End
try to build a bridge
on stilts.
In the effort is salvation…
for they are brothers.

BOY WITH MARBLES

Marbles of all colors
   fulfill a wish, yearning and desire
of that little boy deep inside
   who was denied
such simple
   mundane pleasures.
Bright yellow, red and more...
   now obtained
by the man
   from a specialty shop
counter to the current fad
   for dull and gray.
His eyes delight
   in the brilliant colors
so arrayed
   in a bowl upon his desk –
coworkers stare, not knowing
   their own lost dreams.

TWICE

Twice in her last week
my mother,
that screaming,
vindictive,
demanding
creature in my life
who drove me
more than once
to yearn for suicide,
moved her hand,
I did not know why,
towards me.
The hand that slapped,
which gave concussion,
and forced down vomit,
reached to me.
I watched wondering,
what would she do?
To my surprise
she held my hand
tenderly,
with more affection
than I'd ever known.

>

I cried

Despite her screaming
she did care –

then she died.

FINALE

For the first time
ever,
in my more than
six decades,
I saw my mother
truly powerless
over me.
Powerless to move,
yell, or scream,
or hit me.
Powerless to speak,
it was now my turn
and I did.
"I love you, Mom,
I always have,
but it was so hard
when you pushed away."
She could not speak
nor open eyes,
but she could hold
my hand,
new for me,
and I knew
she heard.

>

I cried.
She did not deserve
the life she found,
the trauma
that warped her life,
imprisoned her
and the rest of us.
I cried for her and us,
said I understood.

I love you, Mom,
I'm sorry,
Goodbye.

REST IN PEACE

She is dead now,
the Screaming One
who once gave birth
to more children
than she could raise
or nurture;
one would have been
beyond her abilities.
She is silent now,
her sharp, shrill tongue,
creating faults
and laying blame,
has finally ceased.
I am relieved
to see my mother go.
She is dead now

and her children
can rest in peace.

ONE LONG NIGHT

"NO! NO! NO!"
The man woke up
from being a boy,
of 9, 10 or 11,
from being pursued
by his mother
to catch him
and control him again,
chasing through streets
of a charming village.
He had escaped the truck
she erratically drove
bouncing over things
unconcerned.
At sixty, you'd think
this would have stopped
long, long ago,
but no.

SCREAMING MONSTER DRAGON

She opened her mouth
and hatred spewed
towards me, about me
continually…
but now I know, not really,
though I didn't understand.
The dragons were inside
screaming to get out,
I merely happened
to be in the way –
little
helpless
vulnerable
the child –
as she was a child
when dragons
took seed
inside her.

POET

Smashed face first
into the ground
I see
tiny grains of dirt.
With these
I make
small exquisite jewels.
I have nothing else
to use.

WIND IN TREES

That soothing sound
comforting echo,
the only one,
from childhood –
weather patterns change
and the wind blows.

I wish it was,
the only sound –
plus children's joy.

MEMORIES BE

Memories can change,
be overlaid,
gain new meaning,
become
a friend they weren't
before,
but effort,
process,
must be made.

HOUSE DOORS

I was in the house
where I grew up
and found doors:
doors of joy,
of love,
and possibilities;
doors my mother
never knew,
never opened,
and they will now
be forever closed.
The house I built
installed those doors
and my children lived
in joy and love
and possibilities.
These doors now stay
forever open.

THERE'S A CHICKEN!

The phrase my son and I
say with glee to each other
when our conversation
 jumps several tracks:
"There's a chicken!"
and we laugh knowing
that our brains
do not in straight lines go
but whirl in circles
with spirals and tendrils.
"There's a chicken!"
And we howl.
It's so nice to know
we're not alone
or mentally deficient:
We Have Chickens
and they fly
as they will.

A FATHER'S LOVE

Love was strong
stronger than a rock
stronger than, larger than,
a mountain
wider than the seas
despite
his dissatisfaction,
frustration
to take it out on Dad.
"I hate you,"
he said at six,
unafraid my love
would waver or crack,
confident
my love would hold us both.
At ten he was so obnoxious
I finally said,
"You don't have to live with us,
we can find some place else,
if you want."
"No," he mumbled low.
The known he didn't like
was better than unknown.

>

At thirteen
he turned into a creature,
hormones,
I didn't know, but
understood so well:
young bull pushing
boundaries, limits
of permission and life.
Love held.
In high school
and college
we were, he said,
"best friends."
Now he's grown
and on his own,
not speaking
to me;
confident,
despite his efforts:
Dad's love will hold
us still.

THE WASP

In the window trapped
between two panes of glass,
it flies up, down, across,
trying to find a way
through invisible glass.
It can't get out.
I won't let it in.
It will die in prison
and I will be relieved.

A RABBIT GOES

Where does a rabbit go
in its hole?
Does it go to worlds
beyond ours?
Beyond human
conception?
Are these worlds
in space or times
like ours?
Or, Rabbit Time
in Rabbit Space,
too far
for us to know
or see?
Where, oh, where,
does the rabbit go
in its hole?

Home!

SUMMER ADVENTURE!

A fine day for adventure,
all the chores are done.
What to do?
Where to go?
Explore!
Walking the creek
flowing to the river,
a hot summer day,
trees leaning overhead,
and mosquitoes.
Around a sharp bend
a car upside down,
a model decades old
with dirt and vines.
Silence of the Dead.
Were bodies still inside?
Or, bones?
Nothing could be done.

BUTTERFLY TRACKS

Paved country road,
evening warm,
hold tracks of butterflies
where they slept
and dew collected.
Wet wings cannot fly.
While drying
traffic resumed:
humans going to jobs.
"Move butterflies! Move!!"
But they can't hear
or fly.
No warning signs,
no passing lanes.
An awful moment
crushing through the beauty,
left behind
tracks of butterflies.

RAIN PEOPLE

Only when it rains
do they come,
when it pours
they dance:
the Rain People.
They're hard to see,
almost transparent
in the rain
dancing joy –
rain brings them alive.
Rain hides them too,
yet makes them real;
rain gives them life
and they dance!
Sometimes,
you hear their drums.
Sometimes,
I dance too.

ON HIGHWAY 50

Clements, Kansas
    with a stone arch bridge;
and general store,
    empty now –
has been so
    for decades.
With zero population,
    the remaining house is empty:
an all too-common story
    of a community that died.
The sunflower crop
    stretches bright yellow
past the trees,
    to Cedar Point, Kansas,
a similar town,
    but with people,
yet still, a way of life
    has disappeared.

BIRDWATCHING AT SUNRISE

I asked a bird I did not know
if he knew
he was a bird.
He did not know, but said,
"If I see another fly like me,
I will know –
and that is all I need to know."
Wise bird,
but from whence comes wisdom?
Cannot humans
find such wisdom too?
and recognize
other humans as human,
one of us, all people,
when we meet another,
knowing all of us
are less different
than we are the same.

BRIGHT LIGHT

Sunflower in a field
on a cloudy day
sudden brightness
among the endless green.

Is the flower aware
of its difference
alone, standing
in deep sea of green?

Does it think, *yellow*,
while the crop thinks, *green*,
as it turns to the sun
its attraction.

Standing out from the crowd
testimony to courage,
bright yellow sunflower,
spot of brilliance in darkness –

as kindness
in a world obsessed with self.

ANGELIC SOURCE

Evening darkness shrouded
and cloaked the land,
colors disappeared.
Trees went black against
the faint gray sky.
The whippoorwill called
from far away, then nearer:
calling each time closer,
then the tree before me.
Suddenly, in flight
it saw me, unusual there.
Shimmering white form hovered,
wings and tail whirring
suspended in the air
examining this creature, me,
and I it.
Two curious beings
intent on the other,
time stood still.
Here was the form of angels
of popular belief,
but tiny – bird sized,
in the air above.
Now I understood:
the form, the source;
not imagination,
but nearly apparition.

REJOICING

It was exhilarating to pull nourishment
   up, up, up into every pore
   and member of my being.

The rain fell and I rejoiced,
   it had been a hot, dry time
   and rain was WONDERFUL!

I watched moving things
   inside their place
   and felt pity for their oblivion.

I danced as the rain splashed down
   and thanked God in His Glory,
   was ever a life more blessed than I?

Lightning flashed and I was not afraid,
   the wind blew and I reached out:
   we were one in the wonder of the storm.

Soon it was over and I contentedly soaked
   in the moisture all around.
   How good it is to be a tree!

DEAD BRIDGE

Skeleton of steel,
   twisted, bent and broken:
by the side of the road
   discarded as nothing,
to be replaced
   by a boring bridge.
The old bridge,
   was a railroad bridge,
and served
   the people well:
buses of school children
   and tons of farmers' grain
had all passed over
   in a century of time.
Now that bridge is gone
   and the world moves on.

REMNANT

Cement rectangle
on barren ground
no other evidence
of hopes and dreams and plans
all for naught.
What is the story?
Where is the family?
Where are the trees,
flowers or driveway?
Cement is mute
witness, all that's left
of once bright
and shining future.
Grass stands tall
waves nodding
under wind blowing
before and after
human passing.

ROCK WALLS

Rock walls
ruins
hint of a house
once
warmth, shelter
now
windblown
stark
dreams dashed
deserted,
the marriage was over,
though
he didn't know it
and rode
to his new life
away
with no time
to turn back.

WINDMILLS SIDE BY SIDE

One windmill turns
in the wind,
fast or slow
the wind blows,
but the turning is a waste:
the pump is not connected.
All that motion
and no water in result.
The other, silent,
does not move
standing powerless
rusted still
rendered useless
long ago;
rural sculpture now
witness of what was
once essential –
only artifact remains.

AUTUMN STILLNESS

There is no wind.
No leaves blowing,
frogs buried in sleep,
few birds remain.
Seasons have changed –
the world changed form:
soon
there will be snow and ice
and then:
regeneration
for a new year –
mirror
of a vast renewal
on millennial scale
when hearts and nations
forget their roots
and Divine Origin.

Then, again: Spring!

UNDER WATER LIFE

Visiting the lake
  I see a road
in drivable condition
  going into water,
old telephone poles
  and rows of trees
line the sides
  where it disappears.

I've driven here
  down hill and beyond.
There was a house,
  with a tidy fence and farm,
flowers all around
  and trees –
all gone now
  under waves.

"Progress,"
  some say...

PLAINS CHANGE

Wind sweeps in
no longer bringing heat
and bugs,
but now a chill
to excite your skin.
From north it comes,
not tropics now,
there is nothing, nothing,
to slow it either way.
Seasons turn
on the central plains
and the wind –
wind is with us
always.
Always there is wind,
without it
we wouldn't know
which way to go.

PROTECTING BOARDS

In a time of new beginnings
James Priddy and his brothers,
the youngest one aged four,
walked and rode
twenty-six days
from Indiana to Kansas
prairie schooner loaded
for life on the rolling plains –
three dollars an acre
of railroad land.
Crates from the wagon sit
quietly in a corner
traveling days long gone,
but still of use
protecting possessions,
though plain and little adorned,
transformed
into a chest of drawers.

AUTUMN FLAMING SKY

Autumn skies in Kansas
    are different
        from the others.
Autumn skies in Kansas
    explode
        in brilliant colors:
Flaming orange,
    scarlet,
        royal purple – deep,
Pale blues and greens
    and white
        contrast and shock,
Blushing crimson,
    silver
        and magenta,
All, in turn,
    illuminate
        the spread of clouds.
Is there a purpose
    for the brilliance,
        such celestial splendor?
Incidental chemicals
    or cursory refraction
        result in gorgeousness,
Appreciated only
    by
        the human heart.

NORTHWARD

Geese flying northward,
flocks and flocks of them –
they know it is the time
of seasons changing;
soon it will be clear
to us humans too!
We are cocooned
in insulating cities,
non-seasonal lives –
unaffected
from but the most extreme
of weather changes.
Geese flying know,
and their streamlined Vees
are evidence
of that knowing,
as we watch in awe
and wonder…

FEEDING CATTLE

The day was cold
sleet was blowing
Dad was sick and asked,
"Can you feed the cattle?"
Inwardly groaning,
I wanted to be snug and read,
but said, "Yes."
I dressed warm in layers
loaded hay and set out.
After breaking bales
and scattering the hay
I sat on the open tractor
and watched the cows
in their enjoyment,
wind and sleet forgotten.
Decades later
good memory remains.
My father died next summer.

ROAD GAME

Crazy teenage boys
playing chicken,
on adrenalin,
late one night:
cars full of friends,
girls screaming,
on curvy hilly
country roads,
up to
one hundred ten
M.P.H.
Fortunately,
no lights appeared
from either direction.
All lived.
One wised up
to NEVER
play that game again.

WIND REHEARSAL

Winter winds rehearse –
blow summer's warmth
and autumn's glory –
far away!
Ice is in the air.
Trees are stripped,
water freezes
and insect life
is dead.
Animals retreat
find shelter deep –
some to sleep.
Humans too
seek warmth,
companionship,
inner space,
activity
and wait.

SNOW DUSTING

A light dusting of snow
reveals contrasts:
an open, plowed field,
every furrow seen,
is more white
than a field of stubble
or pasture land
with standing grass.
Abandoned rail grade
hidden in the trees
now revealed
as a stretch of white.
So, too does goodness
contrast with evil:
as light
is most obvious
next
to darkness.

WORLD TRANSFORMED

Snowfall silence muffles
   all sounds,
enveloping the world
   in peace.
Magic-falling flakes
   float down
lingering in the air
   as if reluctant,
coating all they touch
   a layer of white.
Distant windows lighted
   yellow squares
seem now
   so far away.
The garden sleeps
   and trees wait,
this is time
   for earth to rest.

SITTING TIME

Desperate relief
lifetimes of stress,
six decades of hell,
numbingly welcome
to simply sit,
and do nothing.

So the man sits
in blessed relief;
sitting, simply sitting:
no objective,
no goal,
no action –
to him, amazing –
to do nothing.

But it is not "nothing" –
it is peace,
calm,
and healing.

SNOWY HIKE

Snowy path through woods
leads up, around
and beyond.
The call to "come,"
beckons imagination
and wistfulness.
Winding through trees
up hill, over
and down,
among the grasses, orange
and tan, straying
in the breeze.

The image stays
long after leaving –
what adventure,
experience,
awaits?

DIFFERING

Winter's light bends
into the room softly
where the man sits hunched
over his desk all day,
the work he does is close,
painstaking, and minute.
His wife is shrill
demanding
that he hurry and make more,
and more money
so she can spend and spend.
She rails her wants, as endless as
desire –
does not recognize
her own satisfaction.
The man prefers perfection –
each jewel and each design
exquisite and breath-taking
for the ages!

HE WONDERS

Older now, and wiser,
man wonders
what he's done?
accomplished?
in six decades?
He's worked,
and worked hard,
all his life
since toddlerhood.
He'd like to rest
but doesn't know how!
"Get away!" Some say,
but where?
why?
To not-work
is alien
to all he knows –

but he can watch flowers…

SPIRIT WAITS

Snow covered fields
and rolling hills
stretch for miles
to the horizon.
Clumps and lines of trees
make gray shadows
over prairie
distance.
Winter silence blankets
fields and streams and land.
Growth is hidden, waiting
for that moment
to be released
and burst forth,
to transform
the world,
as Spirit waits
for Spring.

BAY FORTIFIED

Hidden in the hills
   fortifications to protect
the bay, the gateway,
   the city, the golden gate.
Hidden in the hills,
   since 1897,
earthwork ramparts
   continually advanced
past the war
   to end all wars,
empty ruins now,
   abandon spaces
from attacks
   that never came.
Hidden in the hills
   tunnels and pill boxes:
fortified
   San Francisco.

AFTERMATH

Weeks afterward
the party was held
as scheduled:
darkened room decorated
and refreshments –
no school
for this last hour.

BANG!!

Silence.
The students froze.
"Lights,"
calmly the principal called.
"It was a balloon,
no one else is here,"
she explained
to children's wide-eyed fears.
No one is shooting us…
this time.

McDONALD SHEEP RANCH

Here...
in a nondescript house,
shabby, worn,
of five small rooms
"...here is the true Ground Zero,
the place
where the Manhattan Project's
bewildering concoction
of science, bureaucracy, money
and hubris
came to its irrevocable end."[1.]
The McDonalds and their sheep
to points unknown
(the sheep to slaughter, likely),
the cooling cistern caved in
and plastic covering
doors and windows:
"Please Use Other Doors!
Keep This Room Clean!"[2.]
Signs posted
to keep out dust for death
in the room,
peeling paint
and creaking floors,

\>

once the hearth and home,
used to assemble
the first of the line
of Fat Man and Little Boy,
pulsing, compounded darkness
of men's hearts
where the curtain opened
to a light
famously brighter
than a thousand suns unleashed
"capable of changing the whole atmosphere
of the earth
and their contamination
would prove lethal." [3.]
The Age of the Destruction of Mankind,
by our own hands,
has dawned.

. . . .

Will we rise our hearts and minds
above such destruction?
Or, let passion and pettiness
turn out the lights?

COLLAPSE OF CIVILIZATION

"We have to leave quickly, my child."
"Where go, Momma?"
"I don't know."
"What we eat?"
"We'll find something."
"I'm scared. Momma."
"Take my hand."

"Oh! Momma!"

"Run! Baby! RUN!!"

ARMENIAN WITNESS

Tied naked to a tree
sliced into living skin
the national poet,
with four companions,
tortured slowly
for speaking truth.
Their cries of pain
ring through the forest
and the ages.
Unknown men
took barbarous delight
in their agony and screams.
Cowards are not honored
but poets are
who give voice
to hopes and dreams
of a people, a nation.
Taniel Varoujan
was such a one
for Armenia
cut short
before full bloom
but to be reckoned
and feared.

>

To halt the power of a poet
the oppressor cut him down,
too much a threat.
Eliminate the voice,
kill a people
and millions died.
All that remain
are burned cathedrals
in vanished cities
testimony to faith
two thousand years endured
and courage.

AKHMATOVA

"Can you describe this?"
"I can," said the poet
who then sang
of the terror
pain
and suffering
of innocents and children
caught in the vise
of ruthlessness:
inhumane
no justice
just brutal grip
of power, power, power.
Former grace – obliterated
eviscerated
and bleak decades
marched on
to nothingness.

POEM FRUIT

Poems fall like fruit
from some place
deep inside.
Their eruption
sometimes
ruptures through
layers and layers,
years and years,
of pain.

YEZHOV WINTER

Cold –
that cannot be described,
Fear –
that never leaves,
Terror –
that rips one's heart,
These –
our daily bread
and we starve
en masse.
The lines,
the endless lines,
numb one's mind
and heart
as another crumples
and dies.
The lucky ones
are shot.

A SACRIFICE

Liberating army
    from continents away
attacks the village
    to drive oppressors out,
residents hide and watch
    too exhausted to respond.
The battle blazes fierce
    to and through the village.
A peasant woman sees
    a liberating soldier,
a boy, younger than her son,
    walk by and get shot.
He crumples and she runs
    to her dying son,
among bullets she cries,
    mother to the world:
he gave his life for hers
    and she wails in grief.

ME AND MELANIN

I'm known
for the slight amount
of melanin
in my skin.
In fact
I'm proud
to have so little!
SO pale!
YOU
are the opposite
of me
and have abundance.
I hate you.
I will enslave you,
hate you,
kill you
for the melanin
in your skin.

AGAINST THE DARK

In a cavernous hall,
   once a lunchroom
(with balcony),
   now disguised
as a ballroom
   (though small),
not exactly cozy
   for intimate recitation
of poems and reflections,
   but still we tried.
It was a dark
   and drippy night,
though no windows
   would let us know.
Still, we gathered
   and sought comfort
with kindred souls
   against the dark.

ALONE IN HIS MIND

Imprisoned by his mind
he cannot get free,
can not even know
what freedom means.
The voices tell him
this or that
and he believes
because their presence
is unending
and so "real."
The world's "against" him,
Yes.
No one else can know
truly, what's in his head.
He cannot be reached
and struggles in confusion –
why no one else can listen
to voices he only hears.

WHISPERS WASHING

Wind
in trees
rustling leaves
whisping through needles
of pines,
whispering: peace,
soothe the soul
troubled
by stress and pressures
uncontrollable;
I lie down,
let calmness wash
its way over me,
restoring my soul
to be able
to resume life
and function
in the World of Names.

CHOCOLATE BLISS

I sip my cocoa,
eat my chocolate;
éclairs
are the bringers of bliss.
Can life get any better
than this?
In Africa, in Mali,
Ivory Coast or elsewhere,
some child,
boy or girl,
of eight or ten,
is enslaved and working
for my bliss,
uncared for
by their captors,
but I have my chocolate,
and soon
he or she will likely die.

THE END IS NEAR

Did you ever have a friend
who thought the world would end
tomorrow?
The day after?
Or, next week?

If it is next week
you have time to plan
and panic
but don't worry, there's

JUST BEYOND

Birds communing
with the wind
flowing past,
it is late
life is short
and I don't know
what to do
or where to turn.
Turn the world slowly
I want to catch up –
or get off.
There is so little time
for so many things,
she sang
as the wind took her words
to the birds
for consultation
and decision
of utmost importance
to life,
to my life,

>

and the wind
passes by
as will my life
and it's gone…

Who will remember?

What?

ELEPHANT RESPONSE

On a normal day's trek
   over their savannah home
elephants coming upon
   bones of another,
whether family or not,
   stop, observe, gather round
touch, pick up
   and sometimes carry
the bones –
   a connection to those gone.
But only bones of their kind
   not those of others,
rhino or hippo,
   large though they be.

They recognize
   and respond to their own.
They grieve, remember, mourn…

   They know!

BUILDING WORDS

With words he builds
  a life
and lives turn to listen
  to the song
and recognize
  their own.
He rises up to begin
  new singing
after truth
  in words:
words that say
  what others dream,
words healing
  the pain,
words that see
  beyond this life,
words transcending
  all else.

BLESSED IS THE PLACE

In a small office
  a back hall,
  with twists and turns,
  provides a private place
    for prayer, meditation and rest.
The hall was seldom used
  but by one
  who needed respite
  from
    the talking, talking, talking.
There
  he walked to stretch
  and prayed each day
  in his three tongues:
    German, English, Farsi.
He used his beads
  to calm the time
  and finish hours
  of another day
    at work.
No one else
  in the office
  would have guessed
  this use
    for the space.

\>

He was odd,
   they all knew,
   but never dreamed
   the transformation
     to a place of prayer.
But then,
   he prayed everywhere:
   walking down the street,
   driving,
     and washing dishes too!
In his mind,
   and heart and soul,
   any place – and every place
   is a good place
     to pray.
So he prayed
   in the hidden space
   in the back hallway
   of an office
     on his lunch break.

OWL CALLING

An owl is calling
from a tree
too dark for me to see –
Stars are out and night
is slowly closing down.
He is near, I can hear,
who is he speaking to?
Spring too, is new,
has owlish wisdom found
the oak tree near
for home this year?
Through what has come
this honor?
Owl wisely neighbor,
wisdom and protection
to my home?
A blessing from
Owlopolis?

IMAGINARY LIFE

Little boy imagined
a room full of shelves,
shelves filled with books –
just like a Library –
his very own Library,
and among those books
many were his –
that he'd written;
he didn't know how many,
but he believed they would be.
He had difficulties though:
letters and words
would not stand still,
unable to focus,
extreme emotion swings,
but he held on
and decades later
It came true!

FINDING EARTH

We thought we were going to the moon
    but found the earth instead:
a blue-white ball
    suspended, alone and single
in expanse of empty space:
    one home
for one human race,
    we are one together
if we would but see.

AND, THE WORD...

In the beginning was the Word
and the Word was with God
and the Word was God.[1.]
It shall come to pass...that nation
shall not lift up sword against nation,
neither shall they learn war
any more. [2.]
Make the Cause of Peace the object
of general consultation...
Establish a Union
of the nations of the World. [3.]
In Gardens of Bliss...
No triviality will they hear therein
nor any taint of ill –
only saying, "Peace! Peace!" [4.]
Ye are the fruits of one tree
and the leaves of one branch. [5.]

The earth is one country
and mankind its citizens. [6.]

NOTES and SOURCES:

Beginning and the End
Award winning poem from Kansas Authors Club

McDonald Sheep Ranch
   1. David Wojahn, "Tell me if it is too far for you," *The American Poetry Review*, March/April 2010, p. 15.
   2. Signs in the former living room of the McDonald home at the Trinity testing site.
   3. Bahá'u'lláh, "Words of Paradise," *Tablets of Bahá'u'lláh*, 1973, Bahá'í World Centre, Haifa, p. 69.

And, the Word…
The premise of this poem may seem uncommon or even shocking, but it is a fundamental teaching of the Bahá'í Faith. Bahá'u'lláh explained it this way: "It is clear and evident to thee that all the Prophets are the Temples of the Cause of God, Who have appeared clothed in divers attire. If thou wilt observe with discriminating eyes, thou wilt behold Them all abiding in the same tabernacle, soaring in the same heaven, seated upon the same throne, uttering the same speech, and proclaiming the same Faith. Such is

the unity of those Essences of Being, those Luminaries Of infinite and immeasurable splendor! Where fore, should one of these Manifestations of Holiness proclaim saying, "I am the return of all the Prophets," He, verily, speaketh the truth. In like manner, in every subsequent Revelation, the return of the former Revelation is a fact, the truth of which is firmly established....

The other station is the station of distinction, and pertaineth to the world of creation, and to the limitations thereof. In this respect, each Manifestation of God hath a distinct individuality, a definitely pre-scribed mission, a predestined revelation, and specially designated limitations. Each one of them is known by a different name, is characterized by a special attribute, fulfils a definite mission, and is entrusted with a particular Revelation. Even as He saith: "Some of the Apostles We have caused to excel the others. To some God hath spoken, some He hath raised and exalted. And to Jesus, Son of Mary, We gave manifest signs, and We strengthened Him with the Holy Spirit.

It is because of this difference in their station and mission that the words and utterances flowing from these Well Springs of Divine knowledge appear to diverge and differ. Otherwise, in the eyes of them that are initiated into the mysteries of

Divine wisdom, all their utterances are, in reality, but the expressions of one Truth. As most of the people have failed to appreciate those stations to which We have referred, they, therefore, feel perplexed and dismayed at the varying utterances pronounced by Manifestations that are essentially one and the same."

~ Bahá'u'lláh, *Gleanings from the Writings of Bahá'u'lláh*, p. 52-53.

The one message, part I: love, respect and obey our Creator, part II: love and respect creation.

Sources of statements in the poem:
1. John 1:1.
2. Isaiah 2:4, Micah 4:3.
3. 'Abdu'l-Bahá, *Secret of Divine Civilization*, p. 64-66.
4. *Qur'án*, Surah 56, The Inevitable:12, 24-25.
5. Bahá'u'lláh, Tablet of Maqsud, *Tablets of Bahá'u'lláh*, p. 164.
6. Bahá'u'lláh, multiple Tablets.

Index of Titles

A Father's Love	66
A Rabbit Goes	69
A Sacrifice	108
Aftermath	99
Against the Dark	110
Akhmatova	105
Alone in His Mind	111
And, the Word…	124
Angelic Source	76
Armenian Witness	103
Autumn Flaming Sky	86
Autumn Stillness	82
Bay Fortified	98
Beginning Again	18
Beginning and the End	51
Bereavement	49
Birdwatching at Sunrise	74
Blessed is the Place	119
Boy with Marbles	53
Bright Light	75
Building Words	118
Butterfly Tracks	71
Chocolate Bliss	113
Choking Hazard	46
Chopping Fingers	35
Collapse of Civilization	102
Countless Strangers Passing	16
Dead Bridge	78
Differing	95
Dinner Guest	33

Dreamer Boy	37
Elephant Response	117
Emil Driving	29
Feeding Cattle	88
Finale	56
Finding Earth	123
Fire Exposed	5
First Step	12
Fossiliferous House	30
Found	21
Frontier Trail	28
God Created	15
Green Haze	14
He Wonders	96
Hidden in Plain Sight	26
House Doors	64
Imaginary Life	122
Intersection	11
It Is…	6
Just Beyond	115
Killer Boy	43
Kitchen Comfort	39
Marvelous Beast!	7
Master and the Dog	34
McDonald Sheep Ranch	100
Me and Melanin	109
Memories Be	63
Native Proud	24
Native Roots	23
Nightly Refuge	40
Northward	87
Oh, Please!	41
On Highway 50	73

On The Central Plain	27
One Long Night	59
Oven Walking	31
Owl Calling	121
Passing By	25
Plains Change	84
Poem Fruit	106
Poet	61
Pony Express	10
Protecting Boards	85
Rain People	72
Rejoicing	77
Remnant	79
Rest in Peace	58
Road Game	89
Rock Walls	80
Screaming Monster Dragon	60
Silent Teacher	13
Sitting Time	93
Snow Dusting	91
Snowy Hike	94
Spirit Waits	97
Stars	9
Summer Adventure	70
Sweet Relief	45
Table Manner	36
That One Night	47
The End is Near	114
The Wasp	68
There's a Chicken!	65
This Blood	22
This Pet, "No."	44
Ticks Don't Swim	20

Tomato Confession	50
Tree Friends	17
Twice	54
Under Water Life	83
Walking High	32
Whispers Washing	112
Wind in Trees	62
Wind Rehearsal	90
Windmills Side by Side	81
World Transformed	92
Wringer Takes All	38
Yezhof Winter	107

Index of First Lines

A fine day for adventure,	70
A light dusting of snow	91
Above the fence	32
After day, unending	40
Airborne, independently,	12
Ancestor / whose name I do not know	24
An acquaintance	47
An owl is calling	121
Autumn skies in Kansas	86
Birds communing	115
Bones in the meadow lie	21
By age twelve	43
"Can you describe this?"	105
Cement rectangle	79
Chainsaw hanging from a tree	6
Clements, Kansas	73
Cold – / that cannot be described,	107
Crazy teenage boys	89
Desperate relief	93
Did you ever have a friend	114
"Do not leave children	38
"Don't-let-it-come-to-me,	41
Evening darkness shrouded	76
Explosion of glass	45
Farm boy sits in grass	37
For the first time	56
Geese flying northward,	87
He knew he was	33
He was a farmer	29
Here... / in a nondescript house,	100

Hidden in the hills	98
Hills overgrown with trees	26
I asked a bird I did not know	74
I sip my cocoa,	113
I was in the house	64
I'm known	109
Imprisoned by his mind	111
In a cavernous hall,	110
In a small office	119
In a time of new beginnings	85
In silent protest:	36
In the beginning was the Word	124
In the window trapped	68
"Incognitum," / the unknown species	7
It was exhilarating to pull nourishment	77
Liberating army	108
Little boy imagined	122
Love was strong	66
Marbles of all colors	53
Memories can change	63
Middle aged woman	46
My grandmother's house	30
My mother's father	23
New moon… / New month…	18
"NO! NO! NO!"	59
Not only do they not swim	20
Older now, and wiser,	96
On a clear, still day	5
On a normal day's trek	117
One windmill turns	81
Orange orb	13
Only when it rains	72
Past and present cross	11

Paved country road,	71
Peak afternoon heat,	27
Poems fall like fruit	106
Rock walls	80
Sex starved females	15
She is dead now	58
She opened her mouth	60
Skeleton of steel,	78
Skunks mid night	44
Sleeping peacefully one night	25
Small young men,	10
Smashed face first	61
Snow covered fields	97
Snowfall silence muffles	92
Snowy path through woods	94
Spring's arrival has begun	14
Sunflower in a field	75
That soothing sound	62
The boy, not yet a teen	39
The brilliance and generosity	9
The day was cold	88
The phrase my son and I	65
There is no wind	82
This farm I see distantly	16
Through these veins	22
Tied naked to a tree	103
Traffic has passed on:	28
Tree branches	17
Twice in her last week	54
Two boys	51
Unable to write	35
Visiting the lake	83
Walking in the oven	31

"We have to leave quickly, my child."	102
We thought we were going to the moon	123
Weeks afterward	99
When the Master has a stick	34
Where does a rabbit go	69
Who but a sibling	50
Wind / in trees	112
Wind sweeps in	84
Winter winds rehearse	90
Winter's light bends	95
With words he builds	118
Yes, / my granddaughter's dead,	49

Previously published credits:

- Ad Astra Award, Contest # 6, 2009: On the Central Plain
- *Africanization and Americanization Anthology*, 2018: Collapse of Civilization, Poem Fruit
- *Barking Sycamores*, 2016: There's a Chicken!
- Baseballbard.com, 2013: Oh, Please!
- *Burningwood 88*, 2018: Me and Melanin
- *Cosumnes River Journal*, 2018: Finale
- CyclamensandSwords.com, 2013: Angelic Source
- *Dreamers Creative Writing*, 2018: Rest in Peace, The Poet
- *Durando Review*, 2018: Twice
- Edifyfiction.com, 2017: A Father's Love
- *Flint Hills Review*, 2013: Fire Exposed
- JellyfishWhispers.com, 2015: The Wasp
- *Juste Milieu*, 2019: House Doors
- Kansas Authors Club award, 2005: Beginning and the End
- theliteraryyard.com, 2013: Sitting Time
- *Long Island Literary Journal*, 2018: Choking Hazard
- *Orison*, 2006: Dead Bridge
- peacockjournal.com, 2016: Road Game
- *Planet Kansas*, 2013: Found, Hidden in Plain Sight, Rejoicing
- Poetrypostcardsand prose.com, 2018: Chopping Fingers

- *Potpourri*, 1993: Table Manner
- *Puff Puff Prose, Poetry and a Play, vol II, 2012:* Kitchen Comfort
- *San Francisco Peace and Hope, 2016:* Bay Fortified
- soullit.com, 2017: Blessed is the Place
- thescreechowl.org, 2014: A Sacrifice, Akhmatova, Armenian Witness
- *These Trees*, 2017: Tree Friends
- tlaaCollective.com, 2014: Native Proud, Native Roots, Passing By, This Blood
- *Topeka Genealogical Society Quarterly* 2019: Fossiliferous House
- *Vitamin ZZZ, Dream Ticket*, 2019: Nightly Refuge, One Long Night
- *Voices Israel*, 2019: Intersection
- *Wagon Magazine,* 2017: Frontier Trail
- *Whispers Shouting Glory, 1989:* God Created
- *Write On!:* 2011: Differing
- WritingtheWhirlwindReview.com, 2013: Against the Dark, Building Words

Other Books by Duane L. Herrmann
(An asterisk * denotes poetry)

Fasting: A Bahá'í Handbook (comp.), George Ronald, publisher, 1989

Voices From a Borrowed Garden (ed.), Buffalo Press, 1989*

A History of the Bahá'í Community of Samarkand, Buffalo Press, 1999

Prairies of Possibilities, iUniverse, 2005*

By Thy Strengthening Grace, Buffalo Press, 2006 — Ferguson Kansas History Book Award, 2007

Blessings of Teaching, Mirat Publications, 2014

Ichnographical: 173, Delamater–Moore–Curtis, 2016*

Praise the King of Glory, Buffalo Press, 2017*

Escape from Earth: the journal of a planetary pioneer, Czykmate, ebook: 2018, expanded print: 2019

Gedichte aus Prairies of Possibilities: Deutsch und Englisch, Buffalo Press, 2019*

Significant chapbooks:

Whispers Shouting Glory, Buffalo Press, 1989*

Andrew Herrmann Family in America, Buffalo Press, 1990

Die Familia Andrew Herrmann in Amerika, Reckendorf, Deutschland, 1994

Early Bahá'ís of Enterprise, Buffalo Press, 1997

Hidden Meanings in the Poetry of Robert Hayden, Buffalo Press, 2012

Micro-chapbook:
In Praise of Prairies, Origami Poems, 2017*

About the Author:

Herrmann, a prairie poet with a global conscience, and mystic, is a survivor who lived to tell, a writer who exposes lies and a lover of the pure light of the moon – and trees! He is a contributor to several prose anthologies: *It's About Living, Summer Shorts, Twisting Topeka, The Way We Were, Corners: Voices on Change*; recipient of: Ferguson Kansas History Book Award, Robert Hayden Poetry Fellowship; included in: *American Poets of the 1990s*, Kansas Poets Trail, and Map of Kansas Literature. His work is published in print and online in U.S. and elsewhere. He spends time on the rolling prairie reflected in *Prairies of Possibilities* and *Ichnographical: 173*. He has a collection of devotional poems: *Praise the King of Glory* and his science fiction murder mystery is: *Escape from Earth: the Journal of a Planetary Pioneer, or Murder on Makana.* He is now working on a memoir and more history. These were accomplished in spite of dyslexia, ADD, cyclothymia and, now, PTSD.

www.ingramcontent.com/pod-product-compliance
Lightning Source LLC
Chambersburg PA
CBHW030440010526
44118CB00011B/722